Gobind Singh

Worded by: **Dr. Mahendra Mittal**
Translated by: **IGEN B.**

MANOJ PUBLICATIONS

CONTENTS

Publishers:
Manoj Publications
761, Main Road, Burari, Delhi-110084
Phones : 27611116, 27611349
Fax : 27611546
Mobile : 9868112194
Email : info@manojpublications.com
Website : www.manojpublications.com

Showroom :
Manoj Publications
1583-84, Dariba Kalan, Chandni Chowk
Delhi-110006
Phone : 23262174, 23268216, (M) 9818753569
Printers :
Jain Offset Printers
Delhi-110092

Price Rs. 40/-

THE BIRTH

At that time fanatical emperor like Aurangzeb was on the throne of Delhi. To save Hindus from his religious tyranny Guru Teg Bahadur offered supreme sacrifice by getting beheaded. He was the ninth Guru of Sikhs. Guru Gobind Singh arrived as his son when Guru Teg Bahadur lived in Patna. He blossomed into the tenth and the last Guru of Sikhs.

On 22nd December, 1666, Smt. Gujridevi, the wife of Guru Teg Bahadur gave birth to a cute baby who was named Gobind Singh in the due ceremony. The father himself was not home at that time. He was on a tour of Assam and Bengal preaching the holy teachings of Guru Nanak.

"I wish he were here," the mother of the newborn sighed.

"He has been intimated," the nurse consoled her and expressed hope that the father of the child would return soon.

In the assembly of the prominent Sikhs called *'Sikh Sangat'* the new born was christened 'Gobindrai'. The boy was told about the tradition of Sikh Gurus by his mother which in itself was a message of mercy, compassion, love, courage, valour and extreme sacrifices.

Guru Teg Bahadur returned home when his son had grown into a four year old boy. He found the boy playing games with other boys in the courtyard of their *haveli*. The kids were playing war games divided in two groups. The group led by Gobindrai was playing the defenders against the other group that acted as the tormentors.

Guru Teg Bahadur smiled. The kid's game had the touch of prophecy about the future. That was the time when to defend one's beliefs one was required to be a warrior.

The game ended as the Guru watched silently. Then he asked the defender boy who he was.

The boy revealed, "I am Gobindrai. Guru Teg Bahadur is my father." Guru's face lit up with joy and tears welled up in his eyes. He spread his arms to embrace the boy who looked at him puzzled.

Guru Teg Bahadur said in choked voice, "Son, I am your father, Guru Teg Bahadur." Gobindrai was stunned and fell at his father's feet. The father gathered his son in his arms and held him tight against his bosom.

By that time Gujridevi and Sikh disciples had also come out and converged there. Guru saw his wife and admired, "You have done a good job of educating our son".

It brought tears to Gujridevi's eyes.

THE MARKSMANSHIP

Gobindrai was growing up healthily and his high spirits were creating amusing scenes. The *haveli* the Guru family lived in had a well in its compound. The women of the neighbourhood used to come to the well to draw water.

Gobindrai drew great pleasure in playing pranks with them.

He and his band of chums would hide behind the trees or bushes with bows and arrows to target the earthen pots of the women. The boys preferred to shoot at the waterful pitchers for greater fun as the spilling water drove the women crazy with anger. Gobindrai's arrows rarely failed to burst the pitchers.

The women were annoyed at it and they knew that Gobindrai was the ring leader of the naughty band. They decided to complain to his mother Mata Gujridevi.

One day the women trooped to Gujridevi to lodge their protest against her prankster son.

One of the women spoke, "*Biji*, control your dear son. He bursts our water pitchers. Think of the losses we are suffering."

Another said, "Your Gobindrai is not alone. He has a whole gang with him. Our pleadings make no impression on them. Plain rogues they are."

Yet another complained, "Suppose some day they miss mark and hit us on the head which can kill us. It is no more a prank or a joke. Something dreadful can happen any time any day."

Mata Gujri stared at them and said, "Why did you not tell me about it before? Anyway I will arrange to give you all brass pitchers. The boys won't be able to burst them with arrows. Don't worry."

GOBIND CHASTISED

Mata Gujri gave the women gleaming brass pitchers. The women were happy. Gobindrai and his naughty brigade tried to crack the metal pitchers unsuccessfully.

When the boys were trying this Mata Gujri came from behind and caught Gobindrai red handed. The other kids ran away when they saw their leader being nabbed. The women laughed and squealed in delight, "Mata Gujri has at last got him!"

Mata Gujri admonished her son without being unduly harsh, "Son, that was very bad. Suppose you miss your aim and one of those women were to die or get hurt, do you realise how terrible it would be! It is no game at all."

"I won't do it again, *ma*," Gobindrai promised.

The boy was really sorry for causing trouble for his mother.

Gobindrai proved true to his word. He gave up being naughty. His father arranged teachers for his son's education. Gobindrai started learning Sanskrit, Arabic, Persian and Gurumukhi from able tutors.

Along with letters he got training in horse riding and the use of weapons. Gobindrai revealed his literary bend of mind and excellence in the use of weapons. The regular practice polished his talents.

The promising development of Gobindrai made Guru Teg Bahadur proud of his son. He had every reason to believe that Gobindrai would carry forward the Sikh tradition.

The young Gobindrai held a lot of promise.

THE MIRACLE BOY

As far as common folks were concerned Gobindrai was a miracle boy.

Once a famed *fakir* named Bheekham Shah of Gudak village of Patiala state saw a dream that a messiah endowed with divine qualities had taken birth at Patna. The dream made him travel to Patna to check out. After a lot of travails he reached Patna and arrived at Guru Teg Bahadur's *haveli*.

He prayed to Gujridevi, "*Maee*! I hear that a messiah had taken birth from your womb. Let me see him."

Gujridevi suspiciously said, "*Fakir Baba*! I don't know about the messiah you talk about. He is just my son Gobindrai for me. He should be coming here any time. Eat something and take rest meanwhile."

The visitor accepted the invitation.

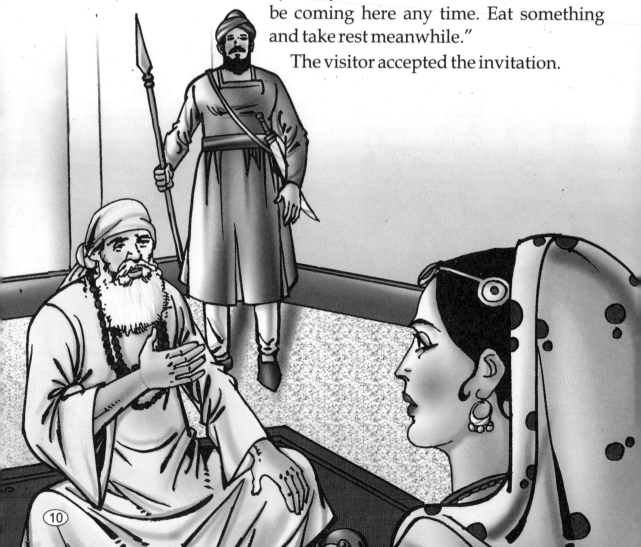

Shortly later, Gobindrai came home. Gujridevi presented him to *Fakir Baba*.

Baba placed two bowls full of water before Gobindrai and said, "Son, touch any of these two. I want to test your faith. The two bowls symbolise two different faiths. I want to see which faith your mind is devoted to."

Gobindrai touched both the bowls and rolled them over. *Fakir Baba* stared at Gobindrai incredulously.

He said to Gujridevi, "*Maee*! Your son is no ordinary one. He will grow into a great warrior and the chief of the faithfuls. He will protect the poor and helpless. He won't be partial to any faith. But he would destroy the faith based on wrong principles. There is divinity in this boy. He will win every heart of the right kind. Mark my words."

Mata Gujri saw the *Fakir Baba* off with some rewards.

KING GETS A SON

At that time Patna was ruled by King Fatehchand. He had only one woe in life, he was childless. At the suggestion of a well wisher King went to meet Guru Teg Bahadur in his *haveli*.

Inside the *haveli*, the king and his queen saw Gobindrai. The queen thought he was adorable. She lovingly called the kid to her. Gobindrai went to her and sat in her lap without any hesitation. The queen thought that she had been blessed with a son. After fondling Gobindrai the royal couple returned to the palace.

They felt filled with a divine hope.

A few weeks later, the queen realised that she was in the family way. In due course she gave birth to a son. Gobindrai had opened the doors of motherhood for the queen. She mothered four more sons. The king and the queen had become faithfuls of Gobindrai.

Once doting Gujridevi put gold *kangans* (Bangles) in the wrists of Gobindrai. The boy felt very uncomfortable wearing them. One day he was playing on the bank of Ganga with other kids. On an impulse Gobindrai took off a *kangan* and tossed it into the river.

The boys who were playing with Gobindrai ran to Gujridevi and told her what her son had done. She went to the river bank and asked Gobindrai, "Where did you toss the *kangan*?"

Gobindrai took off the another *kangan* and tossed it saying, "Right there!"

Gujridevi screamed, "What are you doing?"

Gobindrai said, "*Ma*! Don't shackle me in these trappings. It won't do any good to me or to any other."

Mata Gujridevi was left speechless. There was some latent wisdom in the boy that guided his actions from within.

Gobindrai's miracles had become talk of the Patna town. A Rama devotee Shivdutt also heard about the miracle. One morning he went to the river to take a dip in Ganga. When he came out of the water he saw Gobindrai playing on the sand with other kids.

Shivdutt could not miss that chance to test Gobindrai. He went to the boy and said, "Gobind! Everyone is talking about your miracles. Our King got blessed with sons, so they say. Can you help me see Lord Rama?"

Gobindrai smiled and asked Shivdutt to close the eyes and think of Lord Rama. Shivdutt did likewise and through his mind's eye he saw that Gobindrai was himself image of Lord Rama. An overwhelmed Shivdutt bent down to touch Gobindrai's feet. Gobindrai stopped him from doing so saying, "Lord Rama lives in your own heart and in every heart for that matter. Your mind can project him in any other person you have love and respect for."

Shivdutt became Gobindrai's faithful.

Mogul tyranny was on the rise. Hindus were their prime targets for bigotic torment. It had become difficult for Guru Teg Bahadur to stay put in Patna. He wanted to shift his family to a safe place for security. Hence, he left Patna and moved to Anandpur Sahib with his family. The people of Patna didn't like this but he was helpless. Even after his departure the people continued to visit his vacant *haveli* to pay their respects.

At Anandpur Sahib the training and education of Gobindrai continued. In that matter the father brooked no laxity. Meanwhile, Guru Teg Bahadur kept abreast of the outside situations as Moguls continued to terrorise the masses.

One day one of his followers informed, "Respected Guru Sahib! A delegation of Kashmiri pundits wants to meet you to discuss the terror let loose on them by Aurangzeb."

"Bring them in," Guru said to the disciple. His face had become grim.

Kashmiri pundits entered the court of Guru Teg Bahadur and paid obeisance. Their leader prayed, "O True Lord! Protect us against the tyranny of Mogul Emperor Aurangzeb. His bigotic commander Sher Afghan has issued us an ultimatum according to which we must convert to Islam or prepare to die within a month. You are the only guru who commands respect of all Hindus and native sects. You can talk to Aurangzeb and impress upon him that the religious tyranny is no good. We need your intervention. You are our only hope."

Young Gobindrai was also present. He spoke, "Father, you must help them and protect our faith. If necessary you can go to Delhi and talk to the Mogul Emperor. I think he would listen to you."

Guru Teg Bahadur looked at his son proudly and nodded his head. He promised the pundits that he would go to Delhi to plead with Aurangzeb.

The pundits departed hoping for the best.

Guru Teg Bahadur's promise was no empty talk. He was dead serious about it and he set out with some confidants without wasting any time for Agra because Mogul court had shifted there.

Guru Sahib put up in a garden five miles (8 kms.) outside Fatehpur Sikri, Agra. Mogul soldiers came and took him prisoner.

Guru kept his cool. He wanted to talk peacefully to the Emperor Aurangzeb. Aurangzeb refused to hear him. Guru Teg Bahadur was shifted to Delhi where Muslim clerics put pressure on him to convert to Islam. His conversion could lead to mass defection to Islam eliminating the native resistance.

But Guru Teg Bahadur refused to oblige.

It infuriated the bigotic Aurangzeb.

He ordered for Guru Teg Bahadur and his band to be given such punishment as to frighten the natives into submission to Islam.

Guru Teg Bahadur was brought to a place in front of Red fort in a cage like an animal. In one swish a Mogul butcher beheaded Guru Teg Bahadur.

In that spot today stands 'Sisganj Gurudwara' in the Chandni Chowk.

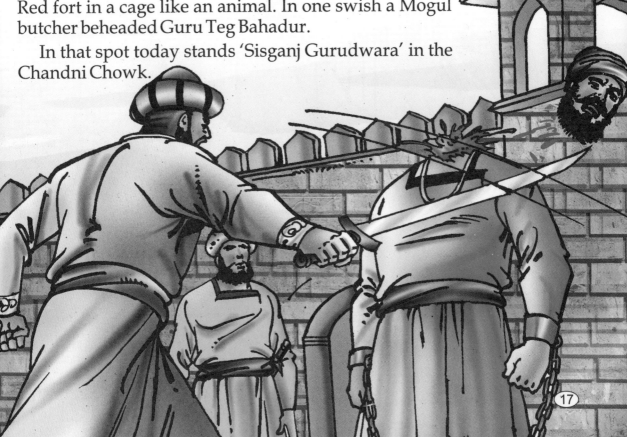

GURU THRONE TO GOBINDRAI

Bhai Jeta reached Anandpur Sahib with the head of Guru Teg Bahadur.

Meanwhile, a nomad named Lakkhi Shah took charge of the rest of the body of Guru. He carried it into his hut loaded in his fodder cart. Then, he set fire to his hut. Everything burnt to ashes.

Gurudwara Bangla Sahib (New Delhi) came up at that spot.

Aurangzeb's cruelty angered the natives. Young Gobindrai pacified them. A large congregation of Sikhs was at Anandpur Sahib at that time. Gobindrai knew that they were not organised and could not be effective.

The Sikh Sangat put Gobindrai on Guru throne on 11th November, 1675. He declared, "This day I add 'Singh' to my first name. You too will do the same. Prepare yourself to fight against the tyrannical rulers like *singhs* (lions)."

All the Sikhs accepted the diktat of Guru Gobind Singh. Guru Teg Bahadur's head was given ceremonial funeral and the last rites were performed.

BUILDING UP FORT

After ascending on the throne of Guru he began the task of driving away fear and cowardice from the minds of the natives. He successfully raised a Sikh army that was well organised and armed. It was full of the spirit of do-or-die. Anandpur Sahib became an army camp. A wall was constructed around the town to turn it into a fortified town. In the centre of the town a proper fort came up. It had a huge *nagara* drum. The drum beat was a call to the soldiers to get armed and to take up battle positions.

Everything in the town and the inner fort was kept in round the clock battle readiness. The soldiers were ever on the alert. Guru Gobind Singh functioned as the religious guru and the army commander. The dual role was the demand of the time and the situation.

FIVE DEAR FAITHFULS

In 1699, on Baisakhi day big tents were pitched outside Anandpur Sahib town in the open grounds. Sikh bands were to congregate there to celebrate the occasion. The tents had lodging and boarding facilities. In the centre of the tent town there was a big top in which sat Guru Gobind Singh on his ceremonial throne with his attendants. A yellow tent also stood there adjoining it. Sikh bands were converging there from all parts of the land.

A *yajna* was performed in the big tent. Then, Guru Gobind Singh stood up on the throne and drew out his sword from the sheath. He thundered rattling his sword, "I want the head of a brave one. Is there any who dares to volunteer to be beheaded?"

It stunned everyone present there. There was a pin drop silence.

The silence did not last long.

A man rose up from the crowd and came to Guru Gobind Singh. He bowed his head and said, "True Lord! This faithful of yours named Dayaram of Lahore offers his humble head for the sacrifice."

The crowd woke up from the stunned state. The tent hummed with sounds of exclamations. Guru signalled for silence. Then, he said to Dayaram, "You come with me."

Guru Gobind Singh took him into the adjoining tent. A sound of the sword hacking the flesh was heard. Moments later a stream of blood came out of the tent. The people stared at it in horror with their mouths open. Many faces turned pale. Everyone felt a chill go down one's spine.

ONE MORE

Then Guru Gobind Singh walked with his sword bloodied and dripping. He declared again, "I need one more head to celebrate this holy occasion."

This time, Dharamchand, a resident of Delhi came forward and offered, "I present my head, O Lord Guru."

Guru Gobind Singh took him in the sacrificial tent. Once more people heard the same 'kisching' sound. The blood stream widened up.

Guru Gobind Singh came out and demanded one more head.

In total he demanded five heads one by one. The third head was offered by Himmat Ram of Bidar, the fourth head by Mohakram of Dwarka and the fifth head too by another Bidar resident, Bhai Sahibchand.

The same ritual was gone through.

JO BOLE SO NIHAL...

The Sikh congregation believed that Guru had offered the sacrifice of the five volunteers to *Maa Kaali*. Guru came out of the sacrificial tent and went straight to a spot where there was huge cauldron placed on a platform.

It was full of water.

Guru ordered a female faithful, "As long as I go on reciting verses of holy Guruvani you shall keep putting *batashaas* in the cauldron."

Then, he said to a male faithful, "And you shall keep stirring the cauldron with *Khandah* to get *batashaas* dissolve in the water."

They did likewise. Guru recited the holy verses. At the end he put his hand up and raised the slogan— *'Jo bole so nihal — Satshri Akal.'*

The entire congregation followed him in raising the slogan—*'Jo bole so nihal — Satshri Akal.'*

The entire big top reverberated with the thunderous slogan.

Guru Gobind Singh moved off from the cauldron and went to the entrance of the sacrificial tent. At his signal the attendants raised the flaps of the tent. The congregation saw an incredible scene. Out came the five who had offered their heads to Guru. All of them were in one piece.

They were in warrior dresses and wore garlands in their necks.

Guru declared, "From this day Sikh faith will be known as '*Khalsa Panth*'. All the faithfuls shall be called *Khalsas*. Each one will get a little bit of the holy potion of that cauldron after which he shall not cut hair and always keep wrist bracelet, underwear, dagger and a comb. He shall not fear death like these five brave ones and be ever ready to sacrifice his life for his faith."

The big tent trembled with the tumultuous roar of *Vahe Guruji Ka Khalsa, Vahe Guruji Ki Fateh. Jo bole so nihal — Satshri Akal.*

A new chapter of the history had begun.

The rise of the *Khalsa Panth* and the aggressive postures of Guru Gobind Singh scared the kings of the hilly kingdoms around. Sikhs were becoming a formidable force under the new Guru. The kings were too weak to withstand the tide of Sikh army.

Those hilly Kings were proteges of Aurangzeb. They discussed the issue in a meeting. One spoke, "We must get the protection of Mogul army as soon as possible before Guru Gobind Singh moves against us. We can't afford to lose time. He had raised a powerful army."

Another said, "That indeed is a matter of grave concern to us."

The third one opined, "We should approach Emperor Aurangzeb and attack Gobind Singh's army to nip the evil in the bud."

The fourth king agreed, "That is a good idea. Attack is the best defence."

THE BATTLE IS ON

Guru Gobind Singh learnt that a combined force of hilly kings was advancing towards Anandpur Sahib with aggressive designs.

Guru rallied his Sikh soldiers and a large *Khalsa* force met the enemy in the battle ground of Bhangani.

The *Khalsa* attack was so fierce that the combined forces of the hilly kings fled leaving behind their arms and ammunition.

The Sikh soldiers made '*Jo bole so nihal – Satshri Akal*' their battle cry and the victory slogan. *Khalsa* army returned to Anandpur Sahib with the prizes left behind by the vanquished armies.

It was the first victory of the *Khalsa* army.

When Aurangzeb learnt about the fate of his protege kings he became furious. He ordered his military governor of Punjab—'Vazir Khan! Destroy the Sikh army and bring Gobind Singh to our court as prisoner.'

Vazir Khan dutifully set out towards Anandpur Sahib with a large Mogul army and laid a siege to the fort. Guru Gobind Singh had got the gate of the fort shut tight anticipating the attack. Moguls tried to smash the gate open but had to retreat in face of heavy arrow volleys shot by Sikh soldiers who were positioned atop the fort walls.

But the siege continued.

Mogul army's siege dragged on for six months. Sikhs were not giving in. Vazir Khan had failed to demoralise them. It frustrated him.

Meanwhile, Sikh soldiers adopted the tactic of sneaking out at night and attacking the resting enemy inflicting heavy casualties. They would run back to the safety of the fort before Moguls could gather their wits.

Somehow Guru Sahib did not like this hit and run battle. One night he challenged to the group of soldiers who were about to sneak out on their nightly raid mission, "*Khalsa* soldiers! Fight like brave ones and not like thieves. Stream out of the fort like warriors and pounce on the enemy to wage a do or die battle. As *Khalsas* set a new standard of valour."

The *Khalsa* soldiers bowed their heads respectfully and promised, "Guru *Maharaj*. We give you our word that we will drink water only after driving away the Mogul enemy."

The next day the gate of the fort was thrown wide open. Guru Gobind Singh and his *Khalsa* marauders streaked out like wounded tigers and pounced on Mogul soldiers. It happened so fast and with such ferocity that Moguls were caught unawares. They fled.

Guru Gobind Singh got Mogul arms and prized cannons as priceless war trophies. Vanquished and humiliated Vazir Khan ran to Lahore to save his life.

How could he face Aurangzeb?

The defeat greatly upset the Mogul Emperor Aurangzeb. He despatched a huge army to capture Anandpur Sahib to avenge the defeat. It was headed by a merciless and tricky Afghan who had a soldier brain.

He believed in learning lessons from the failures.

The tricky Afghan had heard about the manner of the defeat of Vazir Khan. He wanted to move very cautiously.

He sent a diplomatic message to the enemy — 'Guru *Sahib*! May Allah bless you. We don't want any unnecessary bloodshed. Emperor Aurangzeb wishes you to hand over the Anandpur Sahib fort to the Mogul army. You and your army besides your family would be allowed a safe passage out. Sometime later we shall return you the fort after amicable settlement!'

Guru *Sahib* replied — 'Agreed. First we shall send away women, children, old and infirm. If Mogul commander allows them safe passage as a proof of his sincerity then we shall vacate the fort.'

Guru wanted to test the Moguls. They accepted.

Guru Gobind Singh had married thrice. His first wife was Jeeto who had born him three sons named Jujhar Singh, Jorawar Singh and Fateh Singh. The second wife Sundari had born Ajit Singh. The third wife was Sahiba Deva. She was childless. For her *Khalsa Panth* itself was her offspring.

Guru *Sahib* had a Brahmin cook named Gangu. Before evacuating others Guru prepared to send away through a boat his mother, Jorawar Singh, Fateh Singh and his treasury in the care of Gangu whom said, "Look, I am trusting you with what is like my own life. Take care of them. No harm must come to your charges."

Gangu nodded his head.

The boat people got safely away. After that the old women, infirm and children were to be sent to safety. Guru Gobind Singh didn't want any confrontation to endanger their lives since this Mogul army was very large.

A caravan of old men, women, children and infirm emerged out of the fort and went safely through the Mogul army and reached Chamkaur Sahib. The caravan also carried with it the remaining treasury and the precious items.

Moguls didn't get any wind of it.

It the end Guru Gobind Singh emerged out of the fort with his band of soldiers. The Mogul army surrounded them belligerently.

" It is deceit!" Guru Sahib screamed and yelled to his soldiers, "Kill the traitors!" Moguls had not expected such lightning reaction.

The high spirited Sikh warriors pounced on the Moguls and tore their way through the enemy to Chamkaur Sahib.

THE TREASON

Gangu cook reached his home with the members of the Guru family and the treasury. The bagfuls of treasure gave him evil ideas. He stealthily sent a message to Mogul commander, the governor of Sirhind that he has Gobind Singh's mother and two sons in his possession.

The governor of Sirhind at once arrived at Gangu's house and arrested Gujridevi and her two grandsons. He also took possession of the treasury.

Gangu was rewarded handsomely.

Later, Sirhind governor sent Gujridevi and her two grandsons to the Punjab governor, Vazir Khan. But he kept the treasury with himself.

The Sikh soldiers accompanying the Guru family protested against that wheeling and dealing. They were mercilessly executed by Mogul soldiers.

The treachery of Gangu is the most shameful act of our history.

Vazir Khan admired the beauty of the kids of Guru Gobind Singh.

He said to them, "I will free you if you convert to Islam. Not only that you will get big estates and wealth as reward from the Emperor."

Old Gujridevi screamed, "They are the sons of a lion. They would prefer to die rather than accept Islam."

Vazir Khan barked, "Alright. If they don't convert to Islam they would get walled in to death."

"We don't accept your offer. Do whatever you like," the boys said in one voice raising their hands in firm resolve.

There was no trace of fear on their young faces. Vazir Khan too was serious about carrying out his threat.

Gujridevi's dear grandsons were walled in alive. (Walls were raised around them and closed on top entombing them. During Mogul period this practice was used to make some one example of the cruelest execution.)

On the other side, Mogul army had laid a siege to Chamkaur Sahib fort in which Guru was hold in. Sikh soldiers were shooting arrows on the Moguls who were shelling the fort.

Meanwhile, the news of the entombing of the grandsons shocked Gujridevi to death. The two other sons of Guru had also died in the battle with Moguls. To save Guru a Sikh soldier put on his guise and stormed into the enemy ranks with a daredevil band of soldiers. As they engaged the enemy Guru Gobind Singh slipped away in the guise of a Pathan in a palanquin.

The enemy was too busy to take note of it.

The Sikh disguising Guru Gobind Singh was eventually killed by Moguls along with other soldiers. Moguls army departed for Lahore under the impression that it had eliminated Guru Gobind Singh.

HELP TO FAITHFUL

The Moguls very soon learnt that the Sikh killed in the battle was an ordinary soldier disguised as Guru Gobind Singh.

Just then the news arrived that Aurangzeb had passed away.

Succession war for the throne of Delhi began immediately. One of the sons of Aurangzeb named Muazzam was an admirer of Guru Gobind Singh and was respectful of Sikh faith. He sought help when he learnt that Guru Gobind Singh was alive. Guru duly obliged.

With a small daredevil army of Sikhs Guru Gobind Singh reached Delhi to help his admirer. Prince Muazzam was able to defeat his brother with his help and descended on the throne as Emperor Shah Bahadur.

Guru Gobind Singh was honoured in the Mogul court. The Emperor declared that the Sikhs would no more be tormented.

Guru Sahib stayed in Delhi for a few days as the guest of the Emperor. Then, he moved southwards. He reached Nanded situated on the bank of Godavari river where he met a monk named Madhodas of a *muth*.

Later, the same monk became famous as 'Banda Singh Bahadur'. Banda Bahadur set out for Punjab accompanied by a band of daredevil Sikh soldiers. The monk had become a warrior for the cause of Guru Gobind Singh. He raided Sirhind and killed the commander governor. Then he attacked Lahore and put Vazir Khan to death avenging the deaths of Guru's sons and Mata Gujridevi.

Then, he returned to Nanded and spoke to Guru, "Guru *Sahib*! Your enemies have been eliminated and the forts retaken. Moguls dread us. Now you can preach the *Khalsa* teachings freely and without any fear."

"You are really a brave one, Banda Bahadur," Guru *Sahib* praised and added, "The presence of people like you is what keeps the honour of our land and faith alive."

One night Guru Gobind Singh was sleeping in his tent. Two Pathans stealthily sneaked in with daggers drawn.

Guru *Sahib* woke up and sprang to alert state instantly.

In one swipe of his sword he beheaded one of the Pathans. Before he could turn to the other the enemy plunged his dagger in Guru's back near waist. Blood spurted out. By that time other Sikh soldiers had woken up in the adjoining tents. They caught up with the fleeing Pathan and in one blow of a Sikh sword his head was severed off.

Guru Gobind Singh had suffered a deep wound. The treatment was given immediately. He survived. The wound began to heal slowly.

It was the most trying time for Guru Gobind Singh.

THE MISHAP

Guru *Sahib* needed complete rest to let the wound heal peacefully. But it was very difficult for Guru Gobind Singh to idle away time without doing anything. Warrior in him was asking for some action. He began to fiddle with his battle gear. One day he was stringing his bow. The act created pressure on his waist and the wound opened up dangerously. It bled a lot.

The medication was helping little. The wound refused to heal. It was becoming very painful, Guru *Sahib* was only 41 years old. But he knew that his end time was fast approaching.

He issued a diktat for Sikh bodies to assemble and asked for holy Granth Sahib. The holy book was placed by his side.

THE LAST COMMAND

The chiefs of the prominent Sikh bodies and bands had assembled in Guru's tent. Guru spoke to them, "Dear faithfuls, after my death no living person shall sit on the Guru throne. Now on only our holy book 'Guru Granth Sahib Ji' will grace the throne. It will be your guide. Its teachings will be your command and its message your spirit. Follow the wisdom of this holy book and earn glory. That is my last wish and command to you."

"*Vahe Guruji ka Khalsa – Vahe Guruji Ki Fateh*".

"*Jo bole so nihal – Satshri Akal!*" the assembled Sikhs raised the familiar slogan in low-key in consideration of Guru's health.

Guru Gobind Singh gave his last command on 4th October, 1708 and three days later he breathed his last at night.

Khalsa Panth is his legacy to the people of India.

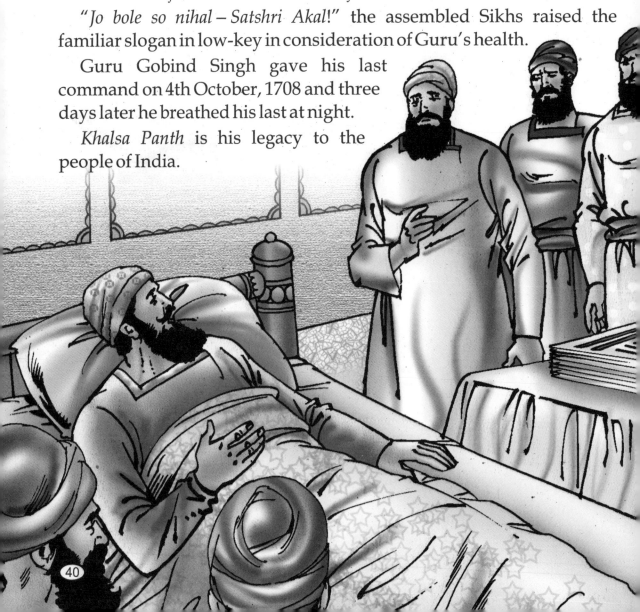